Code-IT Primary Programming

Coding Workbook 2 Choices

A complete Computer Science study programme for Key Stage 2 using the free programming language Scratch

Phil Bagge

First published in Great Britain in 2015 by
The University of Buckingham Press
Yeomanry House
Hunter Street
Buckingham MK18 1EG

CIP catalogue record for this book is available at the British Library.

ISBN 9781908684554

Contents

Contents

How to use this book

Your teacher will instruct you when to use these resources. Please don't complete them until asked.

Each Scratch programming project has an overview page with further challenges that you can try at home.

One star challenges are the easiest and three star challenges are the hardest.

Remember in school it is your responsibility to fix/debug your own code and that is true at home as well. No one learns anything by having someone else do it for them!

If you get stuck you may want to try some of these strategies:

- Read the code out loud. Does it make sense?

- Explain the code to a favourite stuffed toy. (This is called rubber ducking).

- Click on just one block of code: does it do what you think it should? If it does move on and try another block until you find the bug.

- Save your work first. Break long code into smaller sections. Test each block separately. This is called divide and conquer.

Remember even professional programmers get stuck sometimes and have to find and fix bugs. This is normal and will help you become a more resilient problem solver.

You don't have to just stick to these challenges: if you spot something you want to create, go for it.

Bug = error in programming

Debugging = finding and fixing bugs

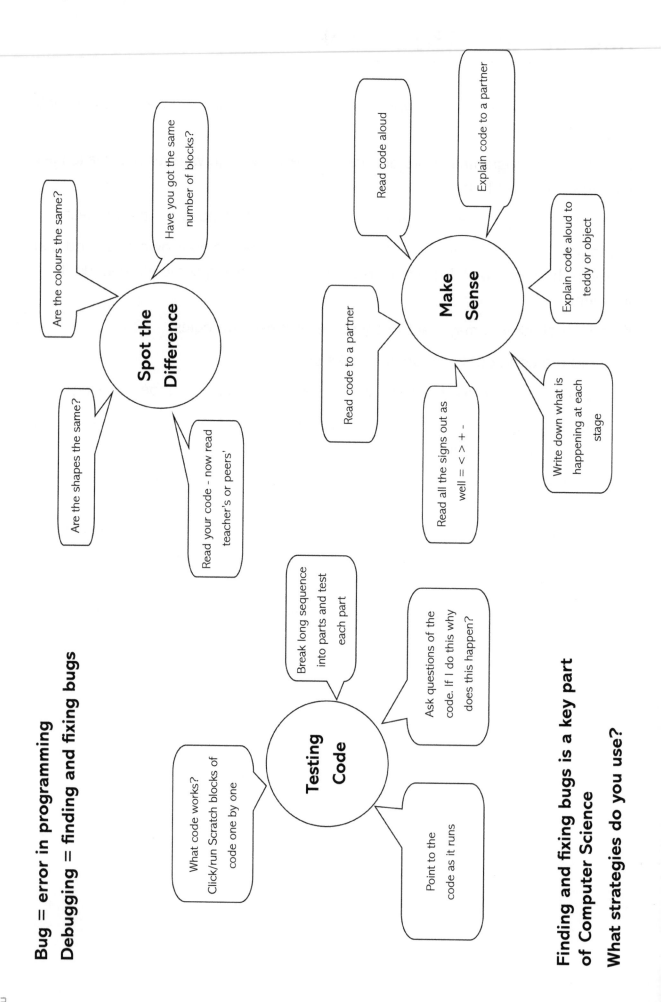

Spot the Difference

- Are the colours the same?
- Have you got the same number of blocks?
- Are the shapes the same?
- Read your code - now read teacher's or peers'

Make Sense

- Read code aloud
- Explain code to a partner
- Explain code aloud to teddy or object
- Write down what is happening at each stage
- Read all the signs out as well = < > + -
- Read code to a partner

Testing Code

- Break long sequence into parts and test each part
- Ask questions of the code. If I do this why does this happen?
- What code works? Click/run Scratch blocks of code one by one
- Point to the code as it runs

Finding and fixing bugs is a key part of Computer Science

What strategies do you use?

2A. Maths Quiz

Create a Maths Quiz that detects if the answers are correct.

Computational Thinking

Algorithm Evaluation

Can you work out the steps (algorithm) that a human would take when asking a quiz question? Can you match the algorithm to the code blocks used?

Computational Doing

Conditional Selection

If you meet the condition one thing happens. If you don't meet the condition something else happens.

Variables

Variables are like pots that store things for you. You can always change what is in the pot.

if   It rains
I get wet
else
I stay dry

Can you think of any everyday conditional selection examples of your own? Write them below.

Challenge Yourself At Home

Ask a parent or guardian if you can download Scratch 1.4 and install it on your computer or iPad. You can find the download at https://scratch.mit.edu/scratch_1.4/.
On the iPad look for Pyonkee.

First Steps ☆ Create your own quiz on a topic that you are interested in.

Next Steps ☆ ☆ Can you add a question to your interactive displays you made in Year 3?

Further Steps ☆ ☆ ☆ Can you write a question that uses < or > to compare the user's answer with the correct answer? It will need to be a numerical question.

Describe your project here

What did you enjoy doing? Did you discover any new effects? Did you struggle with anything? Remember all programmers make mistakes (bugs) and the best ones keep trying to find a way to fix things!

_____

_____

_____

_____

_____

_____

Learning Intention:

I am learning to code a quiz in Scratch that uses a selection (choice)

Success Criteria:	How did I do?		
I can think through the steps (algorithm) to ask a quiz question	◯	◯	◯
I can link the parts of my quiz algorithm to quiz code	◯	◯	◯
I can create multiple maths questions	No. of Q	No. of Q	No. of Q
I can create a variable called score and use it to collect the score throughout the quiz	◯	◯	◯
I can test my code after making every question to make sure it works	◯	◯	◯
I can fix (debug) any errors	◯	◯	◯

Extension

I can add sounds if the user gets the question right or wrong	◯	◯	◯
I can take away a point if the user gets the question wrong	◯	◯	◯
I can change the background when the user gets the question correct	◯	◯	◯
I can change the background when the user gets the question wrong	◯	◯	◯
I can time the quiz	◯	◯	◯
I can add congratulations if the user got all the answers correct	◯	◯	◯
I can make the user redo a question if they got the answer wrong	◯	◯	◯

	wk1	wk2	wk3

☺ I can do it

😐 I did it a bit but didn't fully get it

☹ I didn't get it at all

Teacher use only

◯ ◯ ◯

Record the steps a human would take to think of and ask a single quiz question

1. _____

_____

2. _____

_____

3. _____

_____

4. _____

_____

5. _____

_____

6. _____

_____

7. _____

_____

Draw arrows from the quiz algorithm to the quiz code in the centre

Ask the question

Think of the answer

Compare answer thought of with user answer

Think of a question

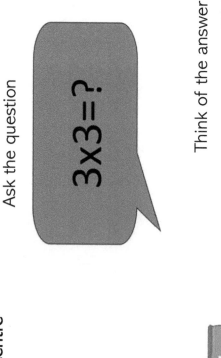

If user answer same as thought answer say correct

equal

Listen to user answer

If user answer not same as thought answer say wrong

not equal

2B. Music Algorithm to Music Code

Convert musical notes into Scratch code.

Computational Thinking

Algorithm Efficiency

Can you use the least number of blocks to create your musical code? Try not to become too loopy!

Debugging

Finding errors in your code. If your music doesn't sound right break your Scratch code into large chunks and listen to them one at a time. Which one has the bug? You can always divide this up even further to help you identify the bug. Programmers call this dividing and conquering.

Challenge Yourself At Home

Ask a parent or guardian if you can download Scratch 1.4 and install it on your computer or iPad. You can find the download at https://scratch.mit.edu/scratch_1.4/.
On the iPad look for Pyonkee. Headphones are a great idea for this project.

First Steps ☆ Have a look at the music notations on this web site http://www.letsplaykidsmusic.com/tag/free-sheet-music/ . Can you convert one into Scratch code? You can use the score help sheet that you used earlier to help you with this.

Next Steps ☆ ☆ Can you discover a way to change the speed/tempo of your music?

Further Steps ☆ ☆ ☆ Can you use your musical creation in another Scratch program such as the Maths Quiz or Smoking Car?

Describe your project here

What did you enjoy doing? Did you discover any new effects? Did you struggle with anything? Remember all programmers make mistakes (bugs) and the best ones keep trying to find a way to fix things!

_____

_____

_____

_____

_____

_____

_____

_____

Learning Intention:

I am learning to decode a music algorithm before turning it into Scratch code.

Success Criteria:	How did I do?		
I can convert the music algorithm into Scratch music code	○	○	○
I can test my music code	○	○	○
I can fix (debug) any errors	○	○	○

Extension			
I can convert other musical algorithms	○	○	○
I can repeat the song three times	○	○	○
I can create a musical card	○	○	○
I can add a beat alongside my tune	○	○	○
	wk1	wk2	wk3

☺ I can do it

😐 I did it a bit but didn't fully get it

☹ I didn't get it at all

Teacher use only

○ ○ ○

Twinkle Twinkle Little Star

Mozart

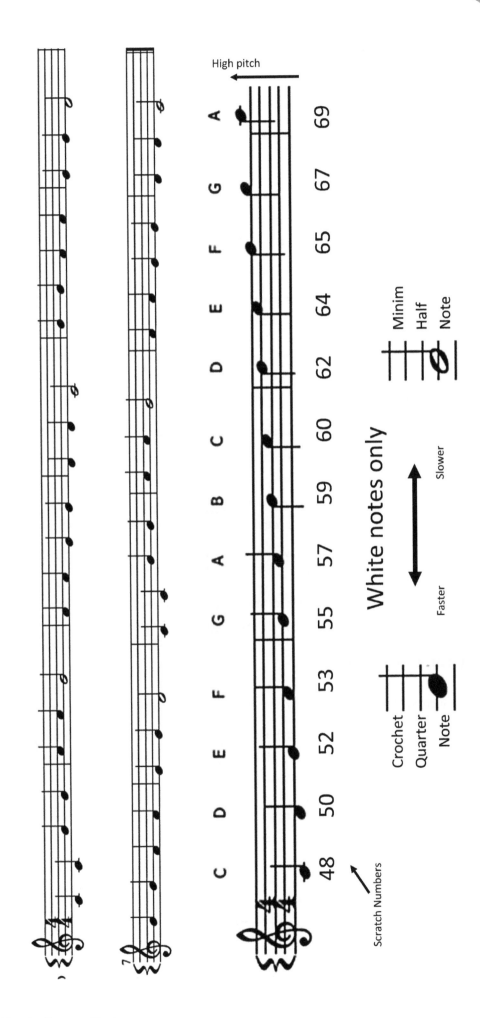

code-it.co.uk

2c. Slug Trail Game

Avoid the hideous screeching sound by making sure your slug stays on the path.

Computational Thinking

Decomposition

Start by breaking down the game into all the things you will need to make and all the things you will need to program it to do.

Conditional Selection within a loop

A normal conditional selection block only checks the condition once. Put it inside a loop and it will check the condition over and over again. I think you have got the idea!

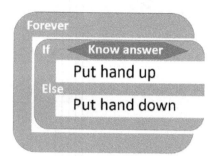

Can you think of any other everyday conditional selection choices which could be put inside a loop?

Would this always work everywhere?

Challenge Yourself At Home

Ask a parent or guardian if you can download Scratch 1.4 and install it on your computer or iPad. You can find the download a thttps://scratch.mit.edu/scratch_1.4/.

On the iPad download Pyonkee.

First Steps ☆   Can you draw your own pen or pencil sprite?

Can you make it follow the mouse? (HINT Set costume centre)

Next Steps ☆ ☆   Can you make it draw lines and change the colour and size of the lines when different keys are pressed?

Further Steps ☆ ☆ ☆   Can you make it stop or start drawing lines? How useful is it to draw things on the screen? How could you make it draw a better picture?

Describe your project here

What did you enjoy doing? Did you discover any new effects? Did you struggle with anything?

Remember all programmers make mistakes (bugs) and the best ones keep trying to find a way to fix things!

_____

_____

_____

_____

_____

_____

_____

_____

Learning Intention:

I am learning to code a Slug Trail Game

Success Criteria:	How did I do?		
I can decompose the parts of the game	○	○	○
I can make my slug move	○	○	○
I can make my slug draw a line when it moves	○	○	○
I can draw a road background	○	○	○
I can program so that if the sprite touches a colour it makes a sound	○	○	○
I can make a key change the background	○	○	○
I can fix (debug) any errors	○	○	○

Extension

I can change the pen colour	○	○	○
I can make a stop all key	○	○	○
I can make the slug draw a multi-coloured line	○	○	○
I can program the slug to say one thing when within the line and another when outside (generalise)	○	○	○
I can write a set of instructions for the game	○	○	○
I can increase the pen size as times goes by	○	○	○

Challenge

I can think how I might improve the game...	○	○	○
	wk1	wk2	wk3

☺ I can do it

😐 I did it a bit but didn't fully get it

☹ I didn't get it at all

Teacher use only

○   ○   ○

Decompose Slug Trail Game

Decomposing means breaking a complex problem up into parts and solving
these separately

What will I need to make?	What will I need to make it do?

2D. Selection Investigation

Discover lots of things you can make your sprite do when it is touching or not touching a colour.

Computational Thinking

Conditional Selection within a loop

A normal conditional selection block only checks the condition once. Put it inside a loop and it will check the condition over and over and over again. It is time to discover what you can program it to do when it touches or doesn't touch a colour on the stage.

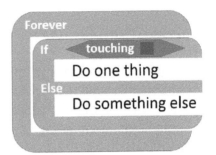

Challenge Yourself At Home

Ask a parent or guardian if you can download Scratch 1.4 and install it on your computer or iPad. You can find the download a thttps://scratch.mit.edu/scratch_1.4/.
On the iPad download Pyonkee.

First Steps   ☆   Set up a sprite to move continuously and steer. Which steering method will you choose?

Next Steps   ☆ ☆   Choose a few of the most exciting inside a loop effects conditional selection that you

discovered in class. Can you create a game out of these?

Further Steps ☆ ☆ ☆ Can you add some form of scoring to your game? Could you use a variable?

Describe your project here

What did you enjoy doing? Did you discover any new effects? Did you struggle with anything?

Remember all programmers make mistakes (bugs) and the best ones keep trying to find a way to fix things!

_____

_____

_____

_____

_____

_____

_____

_____

Learning Intention:

I am learning to generalise (adapt an idea that works to do something similar) using selection blocks inside a forever loop.

Success Criteria:	How did I do?		
I created the move and steer block	◯	◯	◯
I drew lots of blocks of colour on the stage	◯	◯	◯
I created successful code using looks blocks	◯	◯	◯
I created successful code using pen blocks	◯	◯	◯
I created successful code using motion blocks	◯	◯	◯
I created successful code using sound blocks	◯	◯	◯
I used single selection blocks	◯	◯	◯
I used if else selection blocks	◯	◯	◯

Extension

I created successful code using variables	◯	◯	◯
I can think of ways I could use some of these ideas in other programs (generalise)	◯	◯	◯
Challenge I can debug (spot and fix) any errors	◯	◯	◯
	wk1	wk2	wk3

☺ I can do it

😐 I did it a bit but didn't fully get it

☹ I didn't get it at all

Teacher use only

◯ ◯ ◯

Selection Investigation Help

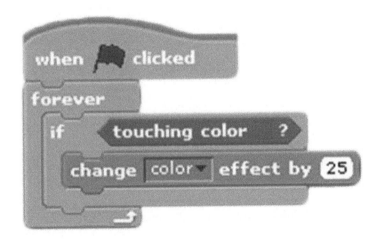

when clicked
forever
    move 1 **steps**
    if key space pressed?
        turn 5 **degrees**
    else
        turn 5 **degrees**

> **Computational Thinking**
>
> Generalisation: adapting a solution that works for one problem to solve others.

Steering and moving Blocks

when clicked
forever
    if touching color ?
        change color **effect by** 25

Single selection block example

when clicked
forever
    if touching color ?
        say Hello!
    else
        think Hmm...

Left click to
change colour

if else selection block example

2E. Teach Your Computer To Do Maths

Don't tell anyone but we are going to teach our computer to solve maths problems for us.

Computational Thinking & Doing

Algorithm Design

Think through the steps to solve a simple maths problem and then convert these steps into Scratch code.

Variables

We need to store all numbers in pots (variables) to be able to use these in our program.

```
when 🏳 clicked
ask type in a number and wait
set number 1 ▼ to answer
ask type in a number and wait
set number 2 ▼ to answer
set total 1 ▼ to number 1 + number 2
say join Number 1 and 2 combined are total 1 for 2 secs
```

Challenge Yourself At Home

Ask a parent or guardian if you can download Scratch 1.4 and install it on your computer or iPad. You can find the download at https://scratch.mit.edu/scratch_1.4/.
On the iPad look for Pyonkee.

First Steps ☆ Can you recreate this simple program to add two numbers together?

Next Steps ☆ ☆ Can you adapt the program to make it subtract or multiply two numbers? Can you explain how it works?

Further Steps ☆ ☆ ☆ Can you make it work with three numbers or solve a two step maths problem?

Describe your project here

What did you enjoy doing? Did you discover any new effects? Did you struggle with anything? Remember all programmers make mistakes (bugs) and the best ones keep trying to find a way to fix things!

_____

_____

_____

_____

_____

_____

_____

_____

Learning Intention:

I am learning to write an algorithm to train my computer to work out maths problems.

Success Criteria:	How did I do?		
I can write an addition algorithm	◯	◯	◯
I can convert my addition algorithm into Scratch code	◯	◯	◯
I can write an algorithm to subtract, multiply or divide two numbers	◯	◯	◯
I can convert my subtraction, multiplication or division algorithm into Scratch code	◯	◯	◯
I can write an algorithm to add three numbers	◯	◯	◯
I can convert my three number addition algorithm into Scratch code	◯	◯	◯
I can test my code	◯	◯	◯
I can debug any bugs	◯	◯	◯

Extension

I can write an algorithm to work out two stage maths problems with only one operation on each line	◯	◯	◯
I can convert my two stage maths problem algorithm into Scratch code	◯	◯	◯
I can think of ways I could use some of these ideas in other programs (generalise)	◯	◯	◯
	wk1	wk2	wk3

☺ I can do it

😐 I did it a bit but didn't fully get it

☹ I didn't get it at all

Teacher use only		
◯	◯	◯

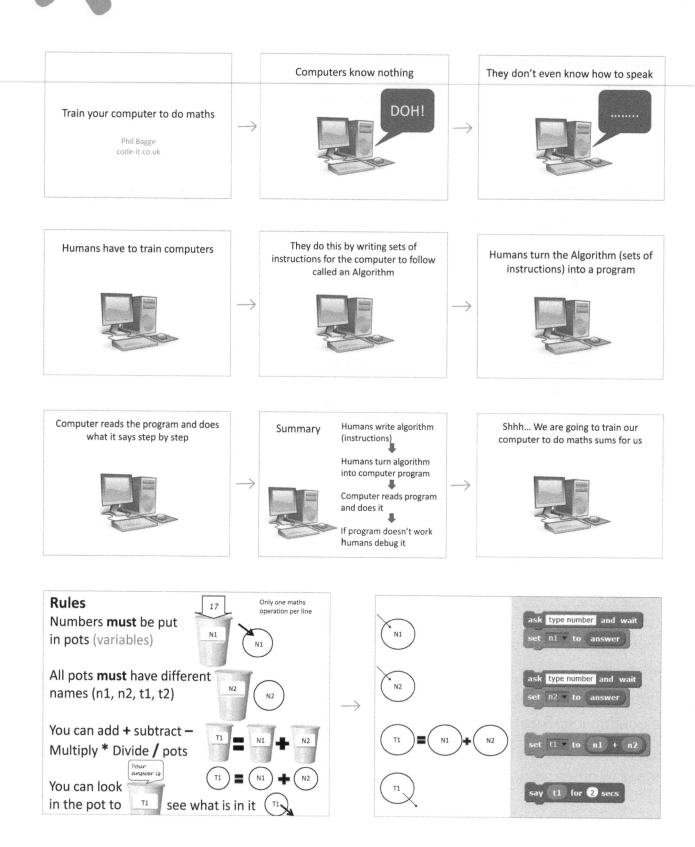

Slides can be found online at http://code-it.co.uk/wp-content/uploads/2015/08/maths.pdf

Teach your computer to do maths algorithm working area

Symbols to use

N1

Put number into variable (pot)

N2

Use variable (pot)

T1

See what is inside variable (pot)

+ add	/ divide
- subtract	* multiply

1. All numbers must be in pots (variables)

2. All pots (variables) must have different names

3. Can + (add) - (subtract) / (divide) & * (multiply) pots (variables)

4. Can look into pot (variable) to see what is inside

5. Only one maths operation (+,-,/,*) on one line

Two number addition	Two number operation other than addition	Add three numbers
Two stage problem	Your maths problem	Your maths problem

Notes